Vibratory Milieu

Carrie Hunter

Vibratory Milieu

Nightboat Books

New York

ISBN: 978-1-64362-031-2

Design by Kit Schluter
Text set in Bembo and Univers

Cataloging-in-publication data is available from the Library of Congress

Nightboat Books
New York
www.nightboat.org

Table of Contents

I.   Lusimeles   I

II.   Carrie   17

III. Per Una Selva Oscura   29

IV.   Oppositions are Accomplices   51

V.   Vibratory Milieu   73

I. Lusimeles

My mind has switched to vertical, just like the dream told me it would.

"The durian is the king of all fruit."

It's best not to leave behind anything you will think about.

Historyless exception:

> I left with a star in my hand. Pointed. Yellow. It was said to be
> performance art.

2-dimensional strawberry pizza

WE ARE VERY, VERY FRAGILE.

"Desire can never be deceived."

The future is a con.

The "personal" as a trope.

Sexual fantasy as a form of worry.

You see that chance exists, but nothing is a matter of probability.

"Name a more iconic duo."

The spectacle, the liberation from the spectacle.

Semaphore.

If you do not repent, this will be the last letter.

> I dream I'm in the sand. Am the last man
> standing. I dream the last torture is poison.

The desire to wear an armor.

MY BODY HAS CHANGED ITS MIND.

If you set your spirit to something, that phenomenon will happen.

When you are linked to everyone, there are no enemies.

Gardens make me think of the future.

In the dream, the word translated as hope was not the word for hope,
but other words that created an inference of hope.

The steps so easily become not the steps.

> Pornographic absence of the symbolic.

They're very anxious now to keep the metal moving.

Theory that economic forces are stronger than political forces.

We may be made of the stars
but are not really in them.

A very successful life inventing alarms.

Box 16A never existed.

"and Robert Creeley of course who like I is tight where
lusimeles goes" —Charles Olson

The fairytale, a nightmare.

We're terrible at predicting the weather.

THIS FLOATING CHAIR.

Vigorous ontological work through the presence of nausea.

Walls of gold, golden doorknobs, not in my house.

A suspicion between us.

(the story in her ear)

The floor is on the walls.

Walls of Death's have died out.

Things that the sun does not look upon.

ESTIVATION.

> Dreams a sort of reality that
> actual reality is in conflict with.

It's hard to understand something that doesn't make sense.

Against gravity's wishes.

An unbroken line of police violence.

The future may not be so rosy.

NEXT RHIZOMATIC EXIT.

When you look at stars, you're looking at the past.

> A spilled box
> of store-bought seashells
> on the street.

The word that came into my mind was stereogram.

The only damage was one lavender plant.

CHRONOSIGNS/CHRONOSINGS

Hospitals are not a place for secrecy.

All the different meanings for "paper."

        Imagining sex anyway.

Seeing my aura around my knee.

"I've taken the plunge into modular synthesis."

The suggestion that the new sexuality is largely about imagination.

                            Myths' odd dual existence.

Writing poetry to poetry.

His name wasn't that then.

The smell of overheated blood.

The poppies are in bloom from the first frame to the last frame.

The subject could change at any time.

> A LANGUAGE IS A HUMAN BEING
> A LANGUAGE IS A PLANT
> A LANGUAGE IS A GEOLOGICAL FORMATION

The gravedigger scene.

The "to-come" as an element of the present, with responsibilities to the "to-come."

Pseudo-flat screen porn.

I dreamt about the word LAST and it was next.

How sound is chance.

The abject's object's objectlessness.

A strange aversion to pepper and ball point pens.

I'd inherited a small dresser, old wood, old fashioned. There was also a lot of taffy.

Identity's I. Identity's eye.

"Pink kingdom."

I just need to accept the new normal.

Life happens and there is nothing you can do about it really.

Dawn as plural.

The white umbrellas were a little too harsh.

"He didn't have a beret on, but he might as well have had a beret on."

Architecture that incorporates messiness
as a component in its design.

But blushing a lot like the invitation meant something else.

She has really good Spanish pronunciation.

Peeling the label off because it is a mistake.

The final script as a collaboration.

      PINEAPPLE ASPECTS.

We're facing what everyone is facing.

To just imagine oneself without anyone around.

Identity's causeway's imagination's
confrontation with imagination.

Our blood would boil on Mars in actuality.

I understand this active wear technically, but I don't understand it conceptually.

They wanted something that they could wave as a banner.

Extracting the melody is not so easy.

When they tell you you're lit, and everybody else is in the dark.

DENIAL IS INAUTHENTIC.

I wondered if it didn't hurt because I was peaceful, or an idiot.

> Geomancy being "the art of divining the future by observing terrestrial shapes or the ciphers drawn when handfuls of earth are scattered"
> —O.E.D.

Refrigerated beach.

Sometimes a father is no solution.

All my dreams last night involved people who were sleeping.

His unalone character stating that she could relate very well to being alone.

"I'll never have soup again."

I say it's the anonymity,
he says it's not knowing what's going to
happen next.

There are words I don't understand.

Hard to tell what was real and what was California.

Words don't mean anything.

If building a house could restore a lost love.

"a sudden and delicious fractal indifference to the written line"
—kari edwards

Betrayed by what doesn't exist.

THE SHAKING IS NORMAL.

The imposition of winter working hours.

"To the robot graveyard."

We remember what we are
when we feel what they've taken
from us.

The news wants us to know that there is a new status for the city.

Trying to process the way to process.

I'll be in the garage.

SEEING GHOSTS WITHOUT REALIZING IT.

Doing the pose that caused my injury, but landing differently.

> the pseudo-object, the sublimated object, the trans-object, the pre-object, the non-object

Sounds like a dulcimer.

This is not realism.

"Who would steal a screw?"

> There are ways to twist the allowed into the unallowed. Changing the viewpoint by degrees.

The ghosts that tend to appear in broad daylight.

I hear the sound of frogs again, but I can never find any frogs.

I understand the presence of a helicopter.

Each surgery has a list of all the instruments they'll need.

> The name tattooed on her back, an angel's name.

It's like *Gone with the Wind* on mescaline.

"Transvaginal mesh."

They took the hands off the clock.

The book is still a technology.

At some point here, he's going to be playing the cactus.

How the secular is religious.

> "once only known by its postal code"

After telling him the terrible gossip I had heard:
—If you heard it, it's probably true.

> The point of one misery is to
> understand other miseries.

Wandering into empty aisles in order to just stand there and daydream into the void.

There's been a drop in champagne sales.

That man no longer exists.

BOUNDARYLESS METAMORPHOSIS'S APPARENT BORDERS.

> The erotic quality in just letting things be
> wrong.

H.D. in my dream last night asking: do you have any #5s?

Whether they are arks or orbs, I am one among many.

"An exceptionally affectionate Arabian horse."

Poems that won't stay in their boundaries, but float here and there and the poet's job is to wander around collecting them.

"I didn't want to hide behind an attempt at ventriloquism."

> "Every act of becoming conscious/
> (it says here in this book)/is an
> unnatural act"—Adrienne Rich

DECISION WITHIN APORIA.

The freeway closed due to a robbery-stabbing and the guy escaping on foot.

I don't want to get my feet wet.

Nearly every day words disappear.

"If Andrew gets up, we'll all get up, it'll be anarchy."

That famous Earth photo.

THE PLURAL OF ADVICE.

We kept moving the road.

No one's lived in the past or will live in the future.

Impossibly difficult stairs that were doorways.

Hesychastic.

> Switching voices between the aside
> conversational voice, that reads as if it
> is not on the page, but (most likely) is,
> and the rhyming metrical lines that are
> obviously part of the poem.

Element Seven. Malfunction.

Something about an airplane.

Time is like a circle that burns endlessly.

I dreamt I got my hair cut by Kwan Yin, but she was yelling at me the whole time.

> This isn't a test, this is the real thing.

The dream building and the real building placed side by side.

I was made by these people.

"We spent hours recording that windmill."

Where the fairy tale's root is located.

Things become less solid, matter starts to fluctuate.

"Strong communities make police obsolete."—Josmar Trujillo

Scratching until I bleed something that doesn't itch, but I make it itch.

Fragment of a whole that no longer exists.

Revulsion towards the other, because the other will one day be oneself.

No one ever says "why," everyone always says "because."

The required path to his room was circulatory; you could only go in one door and you could only go out the other door.

Equivalencies to ecopoetics, how things
are not equal, but equity tricks us into
thinking that that is an equitable
equation.

16

II. Carrie

YOUR TENDENCY TO DWELL IN THE PAST COULD BE
USEFUL TO US.

Wanting something and insisting on it—into the void, forever, alone.

    "creepy carrie creepy carrie"

In the dream, the teacher says: just one class can turn your mind
completely vertical.

                  His sexual noli me tangere.

Terrified as usual.

Maybe I can have my muffled heart back.

We had pigeon problems.

    "and the raven was called sin"

The word "Restitution."

               Maybe everything I dream is geology.

Reading the texts that the texts read.

"had to ruin the game with her on the team"

Then he called the cops on me to make me sign the receipt.

I'm supposed to be moved by this, not using it for my own devices.

A CURIOUS FEELING OF BRAKING AND ACCELERATING AT THE SAME TIME.

Dreamt of a document that is a quilt spread out, and then lines interlaying a poem on top of it and cutting out the quilt squares to be pages of the poem.

"the curse was the curse of blood"

The non-circular, winding stairway.

How light is obviously not solid,
but for a moment it seemed almost solid
and it was gently placed on my face.

Her amnesia could be a blessing.

There are places he cannot enter.

Redbreast, weeping.

"Carrie White eats shit."

"butnamesdon'tmatter"—Alice Notley

Then I notice everything was beautiful, and so vivid, and so bright, and I kept exclaiming "everything is so beautiful," and someone was trying to talk to me, but I couldn't pay any attention to them, because everything was so beautiful.

When I'm with you, I'm afraid.

"Some people can be rational because other people are being reasonable."

Then I got inside and it was a poetry reading on a precipice, I was afraid to move over lest I fall off, and my books and my bag and everything were so hard to situate.

Sensuality is a consequence.

"Did any of you ever stop to think that Carrie White has feelings?"

NOW THAT I'VE SEEN YOU, I'M NO LONGER NORMAL.

There was a bathroom attached, and I went in and there were two very large technicolored spiders, yellow and orange, and I killed them and threw them in the toilet.

"after the blood, comes the boys"

Automated Phone Voice: If you are an inventor, press 2.

"This was the horse we had to use because he was hired."

How you pronounce the symbol is different from how you say it in a word.

We manifest the future by creating its possibility now.

"It is normal to be confused."

We live in the void of metamorphoses.

THE HEART HAS BUT ONE MOUTH.

Magic—by its very definition—must include decay.

"In want of metaphoricalness."—Julia Kristeva

The red lettering has been painted over with yellow.

As we get older, we see history more clearly.

"Who in the world would think that you could get this kind of emotional content out of a parking lot in a shopping mall in Odessa."

"breasts mama, they're called breasts, and everyone has them"

If the symbolism of duality is to show us its own falsity?

Number zero zero three.

"Symphony in yellow."

Then the light turned purple & twilightish and a huge fog came & I thought ooooh it's so low it will go right through me, but it turned out to be more solid than that.

"thou shall not suffer a witch to live"

THERE ARE NO DETAILS.

"My sneaking suspicion is there is nothing awaiting us."

Creating sibilance by separating apart what binds dissemblance to it.

There are places for girls in your predicament.

> Nothing exists. We create what we are
> through the truth of what we have
> forgotten that we are.

Aversive to the landscape.

Pansies, that's what it smelled like.

> "I thought it would be a good thing for Carrie,
> get her to join in with people"

When I say left, I mean right.

Yoga teacher: "Obstacles are not problems.
They are supposed to be there.
They fit into the tapestry."

PEOPLE LIKE US DON'T CHANGE.

Dreamt Emily Dickinson was dictating from beyond the grave, she asked if I would add a dash into her poem, that she forgot one, and that it needed to be in italics.

A person who prays professionally.

The story never told because of the back-story's intervention.

Devotion as a form of consumption.

Time is traceable without being knowable.

> "Carrie I want to talk to you about your attitude, always moping around"

All stick and no carrot.

One of those cities people tell you to like.

Dreamt I was an audience member.

"I erased like 5 different captions I had for this."

CELIBATE CRUISING.

Like having a presentiment.

"Now that's a pretty girl, look at your eyes"

How the sea wave and the sky are both
elements of writing.

During intermission, I wanted to get more golf balls.

There was a point where I thought I might take longer, but I changed
my mind.

I have a small room, but the rest of the house is not mine and I have very
little awareness of it.

"I saw him looking down at me *that* way, and I liked it,
I liked it"

The most ordinary morning in anyone's life.

Biunivocality.

The second thing in a list.

25

As if the self were an herb you could gather.

I'm not a parade person.

ONE DAY THE INVISIBLE MANIFESTS.

The poet will die.

"Pimples are the lords way of chastising you"

Nothing's really happened until it's been described.

Prediscursive or postdiscursive poetics.

If true consciousness lies below the conscious level.

A duality that means both of us.

A small percentage of men only respect you if you yell at them.

The free packets of coffee stopped showing up.

Images can be easily manipulated depending on the music.

The cats jumped in my lap, telling me their magical name, I'd pet them for a while and then they'd jump back out the window.

Dream about eating rose petals.

MASTERPIECES ARE HYPOTHESES.

You are never alone on a plane.

Everything is allowed. Nothing is possible.

Music performs time.

I felt sort of destroyed.

Cement that bends.

"11% of girls are deflowered in a car."

So many psychic moments today, all having to do with tabulation.

Doing nothing becomes an art here.

"In the absence of stealable food, best friends."

The economy is scary.

The chairs with their backs to one another.

> To have come to this through the process
> of its own process instead of another's.

I am Carrie scheduled for Thursday but accidentally came on Tuesday
and there happens to be a Carrie scheduled for Tuesday, but she is not
here, so I am her.

Above the window is written like graffiti, Dragons Love You—

Trying to remember childhood feelings in my body.

Nothing belongs to anything and anything doesn't exist.

Fear must be banished. Fear of thinking, fear of being happy.

"To end police violence, we must end policing
as we know it."—Keeanga-Yamahtta Taylor

THE REVERSAL OF THE REVERSAL.

> Evidences of animal suicidality.

We stop at the motel.

The sunlight is a mirror.

My nostalgia is starting to bore me.

III. Per Una Selva Oscura

Spectrality's *Spectre*.

Back then I could survive an exhaustion by fighting it, by refusing to cave in.

He was so pissed, he didn't read, but told this long drawn out story about finding a praying mantis in the bathroom of his temp job.

PEOPLE STOP WALKING AND JUST STAND.

It's the refusal of subterfuge. It gives way to lucidity.

I'm reading about the differences between juices the way you read about wine.

The power of not saying things, but influencing them anyway.

She has written requesting to withdraw her resignation.

We're in spiral mode.

There is sound.

"The majority of women habitually read themselves into fallen stances; their habits of reading were thoughtless, intemperate, self-indulgent, and consequently, self-perverting." — *Sylvia Plath and the Mythology of Women Readers*

Reverse tears.

The blue ticket counter.

Privacy is not a certainty.

The aesthetics of the bus.

Dreamt we were impersonating either oranges or orange juice or something orange, and a bunch of us were crammed into a human-sized crate.

> The similarity between "leaf" and the
> "hood" of the snake in Sindhi.

It's a feedback loop & nobody knows where the loop stops.

Can't I just be afraid without a definite object?

This is in a hospital.

The new "web" that is just coffee dates.

I COLLECT SITUATIONS.

How gender annuls the universal.

There is someone pounding on a door so hard I wake up,
and no one is pounding on a door.

"Such a difference between what you dream about and what's really there."

The past having fallen out of "tense."

The way we want everything to have a gender if it is a concept,
but we don't want people or things to have a gender.

Abandoning surfaces or abandoned to surfaces.

The water here is nicely scented.

How glamour became grammar.

BODILINESS HIDING IN SEXUALITY.

The energy exchange without the exchange.

Yoga teacher: There are no bad feelings or good feelings, just information.

"Had she lived, I could have solved the mystery of this resonance."

In a panic because I see no menu anywhere.

"A mood for sure."

We can ask DNA to change the circuitry for us.

I can make her appear or disappear at will.

The influence the original sound exerts on the clone body.

> Desire is an emptiness that
> desires an emptiness, which turns
> in ways that leave the illusion
> displaced or perfectly placed.

We came here before we were born.

I'm wearing Nightfall.

"Your subjects may be more adaptable than you realize."

No seven second delay here.

A man comes in and turns off the power, but the music continues.

Then later, I realize I don't even have to go up the stairs, if you just stay there, the whole floor moves.

STILL LIFE WITH STUCK THINGS.

As if outside of the space where God resides is a space where God does not.

"Say goodbye to the sleigh."

A lot of _____ I want that I make up the existence of.

     lemon-colored sunlight

"Happiness is forgetfulness."

He wanted me to read this poem, this amazing poem, and I did and it was written on this old man's clothes, so I was reading his shirt and then I wanted to read his pants so he took them off and even though he was really old, there was this really nice smell to his pants, like cologne.

"THERE IS NO PROOF THAT YOU EXIST."

               "The writer's having lived in the writing the reader in turn lives in."—*The H.D. Book*

The book as future, futurity.

The complaint questions a particularity that misses the point.

The ancient vegetarians Porphyry and Eustathius.

How debt is private.

"I live by the sky & die by the sky."

We all kill what we love.

There is no anonymity.

I TELL HIM I WANT TO HEAR HIS DREAMS AND HE TELLS
ME THREE.

"The handwriting was identical."

Overheard: "He only made me cry twice."

Someone who comes up to the stage
and explains all the inside jokes.

Traveling forever, never arriving.

I knew there was something scientific going on when
I saw the boy with the alligator that had human teeth.

Nongendered, until we choose it.

"Why can we never do anything at the most important moments?"

There is so much I don't need. I don't even need my body.

I go and stand in every room that I am going to lose, and it is all of them.

As I am writing something with a lavender pen, the pen is running out, so what I'm writing is illegible.

> "Endure all dualities with calmness, while trying at the same time to remove their hold."—Sri Yukteswar Giri

In my drunk cooking segment, I made a lot of wrong choices.

Inertia is just a process of things getting very far away from each other.

"One should try everything."

Watching the band practicing songs they will not play.

"The certainty that I heard someone calling me."

Random placement of things in an unordered order.

> A deeper blue vs a lighter blue.

A NEGATIVE INFINITY.

I can't find my flashcards.

Continuous partial attention.

Dorian Gray's other picture.

Just like a real robot.

"Everything means something to someone."

The yoga teacher that tries to speak with a peaceful intonation, but it comes out in staccato inflections which sounds like suppressed anger.

I CAN'T DECIDE WHICH DIRECTION TO TURN SO I JUST KEEP TURNING.

They eat so many fireflies that they themselves begin to glow.

Finding time in patches and how there are two times & they find each other irrelevant.

"She didn't try to resist and handed me the letter."

Only talk to the Phantom if you are talking back.

"Because in this sorry world, the night undoes the work of the day."

We have to be careful about describing motivations.

"We have to drink in silence."

The sound of the faucet turning off.

I tell them that I do not sleep near the windows.

"No one's ever stilled his hunger with manners, my dear."

The dream is in slow motion, danger-style, and all the sudden there is a cheetah there.

The anti-poetic voice as a defense.

Stranded in the moment passing between us.

A basement room that you step down into and is in the back of the building.

"And I'd say to God do your best and crush us."

Space touches itself and replicates itself and becomes.

I had put my heart outside so I'd have a place to sit.

Daybook of following Robert
Duncan following H.D.

SEXUALITY'S COUSIN.

Dependent parts that are also an independent substance.

How the hot water heater accidentally got turned to tepid.

The word bandolier.

He stayed alive by keeping still and only moving to follow the shadows.

Trying to find North, moving around in a circle, clockwise.

We move through the amorphous holy, strands of which stick to our clothes.

"HANSEL'S ARRIVED."

We're not always fucking our parents, sometimes we're just fucking people.

Masked robbers, gun silencers, large quantities of gold.

"It's very convenient, isn't it, for a white person to have philosophical reservations about the effectiveness of violent black resistance?"
—Shannon Sullivan

The bell becomes machinery.

We still have some firsts left.

"The illusion of health is not health."

Having sexual fantasies with your eyes closed is not "meditation."

All day I've been doing that thing that cats do,
staring at corners for hours, utterly motionless.

Poetry as a replacement for homosexual desire.

Things are different here and I'm not sure I understand what to do.

Sometimes you mean to do one thing and you do something completely
different.

Collecting things to discard them.

> One's self-identity working against
> becoming a self.

If reversibility is duality's antidote or simply a more fluid duality.

Passively listening with attitude.

Fusing what you are not allowed into with what you are.

Not personal ambition, but issue-ambition.

"She already belonged to the unseen world."

I imagine you standing solitary in the conduction.

We'll have to make up a story about him.

The public depends on the private's
existence.

Places where things have come unglued.

"I wasn't even tempted to speak of the letter."

Everyone looking for the turquoise scarf.

If I was one of those types, but I never am.

Finally, a duplication that is not a duplicity.

"More women than men use the death grip."

I EMPATHIZE WITH COLORS.

And in this unnamed *in media res* there is another, but this one is named.

What time does with itself outside of us.

"Yes, I like to be alone at night."

If the earth is a diction.

"Here for the moth memes that came upon us out of nowhere."

A list of dualities in which all the dualities are the same things.

I CAN BE THIS WHAT I AM WHEN I AM WHAT I WANT TO BE, ONLY IN MEMORY.

"A priest has no opinions."

Feeling caught up in the concept of a self.

"If you're a bird, I'm a bird."

The energy given is meant for an inner work, but it is given up into the outer.

If assertiveness destroys one's own sense of wildness.

A new taxonomy.

"We inhabit a world of intersecting secrecies. We live and die in the place where those secrecies meet."

People can die of suicide and never make it into the statistics.

Now "I" is someone else.

These are not Utopia instructions.

Adjacencies towards friendship.

"Just thinking about giraffes makes me angry now."

> The trope of seriousness. Or. The irrational's relation to the rational is irrationality's importance to itself.

People who have stories in them.

On the outskirts of narrative.

Nostalgia for the present would be an empty space.

MEADOW HOLES LIKE DONUT HOLES.

There's exodus and there's Exodus.

The choral reaches up. You see their arms hovering.

I like certain things, like piano music.

Pinpoint experience and it exists.

Discursion is prediscursive.

Women have to wear mustaches. And pears.

Three psychiatrists quit in rapid succession.

"A dialogue no one ever has, not even in his heart."

> Let's plan to never do the same things
> for the sake of a nostalgia.

"Light is the first animal of the visible."

Not the language of the body, but the language on the body.

The only chance to read is the only chance to be.

"The relationship between me and the other isn't symmetrical."

A psychological condition that creates an unquenchable thirst.

> Dream voice: "How do you get the
> bright wings off the table?"

Montage practice.

All disease is on a continuum.

A room of one's own is a temporality.

"It's like we're in a mirage together."

I CAN SEE THE LIGHT AND IT'S A DISCO LIGHT.

What the body cannot process, it echoes.

A preference for paragraphs today.

How unity's specificity splits.

> None of the parts have any meaning,
> yet you understand the meaning
> when they're all put together.

The shoe belongs in the lake now.

"secret/ knob/ thistles/ thanking"—Carrie Hunter

All the pretty girls have soot on them.

What's happening over here is in conversation with what's happening over there.

If only the tension in the drama
could just be a conversation
that shows a philosophical point of contention,
rather than just people chasing one another.

"If I learn too much I won't always be happy."

My debt or his debt was eradicated by the decision.

My New Year's resolution is to have nightmares.

"As dungeons go, this one's not so bad."

A gloomy mood triggered by a bright
red book.

What I remember of her is about precisely three memories.

Hopefully the young ones will get their sense of direction from their
mother.

"The disease is human emotion."

Once I escape out the window,
I see a bookcase with books,
and there are books everywhere,
on the balcony, on the trellis, in the light well.

"Because the more you learn, I think the more depressed you are."

Sexuality's relation to remoteness.

PROOF OF AN EMOTION.

A voice told me wake up, you have to go
to the hospital, your body is collapsing in
on itself, so I did, I woke up and I went to
the hospital, but it was still in the dream.

A coin that means later.

Dream of larva nesting in my hair, eating away at my crown chakra.

The counterpoint's hyper disengagement.

Sleep stealing.

"All those things that might tempt us to feel again."

He puts me in an induced coma and in ice, but I wake up and am back the same way and the same problems happen and I realize I have to die and am pretty depressed.

Typical Marxist fear of the mystical.

"We're going to need more holy water."

A goth music hymnal book.

HAPTOCENTRICISM.

The best line is a concision.

Or a bird comes.

Watching the lit candle in the next-door neighbor's bathroom.

Keep seeing the color yellow everywhere
and I see a woman in yellow,
maybe a "vision" woman, like an angel,
but she is in a yellow raincoat with a hood.

People drink more coffee when it's cold.

"It is body worship which becomes sex."

Then I see naked people and I wonder if I'm naked.

"A VESTIGIAL WORD FOR A FEELING YOU'VE NEVER FELT."

The mythology of quiet houses.

I went into my bedroom and was flipping through all my papers and couldn't find things and it was messy, I was in a panic, and somehow everything was white, the paper, the bedspread, the carpet, and the whiteness was not purity or beauty but representative of all this chaos blending into itself.

I can't feel what I feel, but I know I feel it.

You pull and I'll pull back.

Surgery to get my circumcision put back on.

A combination of the unexpected and the inevitable.

The problematics of using the word "psychosis" to describe either lesbianism or poetry.

Rain music misinterpreted as actual rain, and I dream of a rain fairy coming to me and saying "about," and she is calling me.

IV. Oppositions Are Accomplices

Wandering through the murky adjunct pool.

We are to live in booths.

I have a sequence of events that I will create a sequence for.

That it is spells, but that it is words which is what defeats the enemy, the demon, or whatever.

Later the weather starts to change, it gets cooler and the alligator goes back down into the sewer through this convenient hole.

She wants to trick the beginning into addressing itself again.

"The 'prison industrial complex', the tawdry if tacit alliance between capitalism and a structurally racist state."—Angela Davis

Not order different from anti-order.

How to keep customers in the store.

"Sense offense."

Times overlaid onto other times, which create a reality whose time centers in an even different time.

Never interested in tennis shoes.

YOUR VICE BEING GIVEN TO YOU.

This shaggy pothead bookstore poet who kidnaps two women and injects them with a memory serum to make them talk about their personal histories.

The middle lowers and then rises.

A widespread practice of non-compliance.

"Nobody's straight, what's straight?"

DEFINITE GOSSAMER.

Dreamt we were assigned a bookstore, and it was cool that we had a bookstore, except everyone had a bookstore, so it wasn't that special.

"This is a choice not dictated by emotion."

> Supposedly back then
> they made lists and lists
> of lists all about organizing
> consciousness.

Off-label use.

Mad crush on meaninglessness.

Not afraid of extreme A-lines.

I said "I demand that you pull over" and he wouldn't,
I kept saying the word "demand" over and over, demand,
I demand: but the word's power was useless language
and he kept ignoring me.

The problem isn't actually that hard to solve.

"Because this is a choice within a very strict set of parameters."

"Don't become a global pariah."

The clock in my dream keeps saying 2AM every time I look, but it is light out, so how could it be?

FORGOT THE MOON EXISTED.

Just do what you like to do.

This idea that well-being
is possible.

I am braiding phrases from books of history into my hair, books of history that are about my history, geographical history mixed in with my emotional history.

All attempts at truth or knowledge are attempts at power.

When I say what I really want to say, I say it very softly.

This is almost magic.

Secret signals or codes the dream gives you to tell you that you're dreaming, which only seem obvious later.

I try to bring my dream-dog to class, a whole dream of things in the wrong places.

How the other is not an "other" because "I" don't exist.

Sexy Ferris wheel.

An unconditional end to a future choice.

If the dreams I don't remember, I don't remember because they have nothing to do with me; they are just floating through in the dream-ether.

Covered up in transparencies.

Dream of writing down my dream, but I can't remember my dream.

The voice the notes obey.

Synthetic biology.

"I THINK THINGS THAT MOVE ARE BEAUTIFUL."

I have taken part in some sort of anarchist destruction, the burning down of a building, but have left everything important to me in the building, so it is lost, destroyed.

"You can ignore love, but then you wake up in the middle of the night and so forth" —Slavoj Žižek

"Fear of flying isn't your only problem."

Cyclical time's connection to oracle.

The problem of disjunctive binarism trying to eradicate the problem of disjunctive binarism.

A border that is an ambiguity.

A bird combined with the backgroundless background.

All plants are roughly two-thirds sugar.

Perfume chess piece.

Dream I am tying my shoe and my estranged lover walks in. I see his dirty old shoes and panic, so I just stay down there, doing things related to my feet.

The zombies are waking up.

"Go ahead take your clothes off, hurry up."

The real subject not alluded to.

The mandala's insistence on
boundaries.

Windows are escapes or entrances and appear and reappear in dreams.

THE BEAT OBEYS ITSELF.

Because we have to be secret, he has sex with a pirate.

If your oppression has a past that includes a nostalgia.

Affected by what does not yet appear to be a thing.

Tone leading suicide moments.

Post shiitake mushroom nausea.

"Nationalism is wretched."—Roberto Bolaño

The communal pronoun.

Inverted word order/inverse floater.

My computer just used an adverb.

Clock ticking.

Dying all the time, everyday we're dying, but one day the process will end.

WE DO NOT COOPERATE WITH BELIEF.

He's running out of foreclosed properties.

The poet's mouth open between lines, performing her reading while staring at the audience intently in a sort of sensual demand of the audience.

"Girls have energy, vitality."

The ceiling was peeling back in this one room with a washer and dryer, and then I saw the person above lift up the ceiling, from their floor, and throw in some clothes into the washer from above.

I already have a bowl of olives, every table has olives.

"You exist to continue your existence."

The one born before Lilith.

Teaching in this room made out of cake, the walls are pink frosting, everything is pink, and everything is easy, easy, easy.

ALL I WANT IS WHAT I CAN USE AND BEND.

There are limits to the enthusiasm that you can express.

"We all play the fool sometimes."

Everyone left their shoes at my house.

A chora is a receptacle and an interval.

What the narrator cannot fully recall.

Making makeshift keys out of carrots.

Reality is a music.

Relegated to a life of horror.

"THE LESS WE SAY ABOUT IT THE BETTER."

The darkness creates in me a panic, but I sort of like it.

There are dumpsters in this scene.

A memory leaking.

Notebooks are for spying.

"There are theories."

God is not permission.

He is at the reading he can't read at, at the time he is supposed to read, and everybody is confused; Why is he here if he can't read here?

A broken heart, but a broken heart that is a relief.

The Phallus, capitalized and abstracted.

"It was time to take a look at everything that I'd been taught to believe."

I say I don't need it, but he says here, take it.

I'm not surprised, but someone somewhere might be surprised.

"Before the inferno, I had a light heart."

Time as we know it, but time muted.

Whether or not my life is just a collection of texts.

The subject doubled because the real subject itself is unmentionable.

What you just did in my daydream was kind of dramatic.

In real life I make a lot of typos.

HOW WINDOWS ARE INEXORABLY BOUND UP WITH TIME.

The California deluge was caused by an atmospheric river.

But I did find a few open doors to stand near.

So angry at trash.

"The time lock is engaged."

There also was bicycle grease everywhere in the pool water
because so many other people were doing the same thing.

The voyage to the nuthouse being a spiraling voyage upwards.

"Not a job, it's an art."

Everything we need to survive is in a very limited supply.

Stella's dove having surpassed Catullus's sparrow.

A MYSTICISM ABANDONED FOR A PRACTICALITY.

"There's a woman down the street calling your name."—person on
the street

"Have you noticed how nobody works anymore."

My first purgatorial action is inertia.

I was in a tiny room that I had a key to, like a hotel, but not a hotel.

I was here before, when I was supposed to be here, but I'm not supposed
to be here now.

Mano a mano.

"I suspect that sadness is not compatible with sadness."

I couldn't remember his name, and so in the moment of trying to remember I just said any name, and he glared at me.

Everyone is smiling today.

"Turbines primed."

Reasons why authenticity fails.

Bisexuality not quite its own culture.

THERE IS NO YOU HERE AND THERE IS NO WANT.

Changing their communication practices.

This is a terrible movie.

That which the mimic mimics and that which the mimic leaves unsaid.

I was standing there talking to people, but also hiding.

Feeling extremely specific.

Maybe because it's such a common name.

The unrepresentable.

The fear of the other's existence overtaking one's own.

Not Robert Duncan's birthday.

I brought all these breakfast items over into the dream from the last dream where they were giving them out for free.

"The end of telos, of sexuality."—Judith Butler

"When immigrants come, they bring their food."

Not my year.

The corpse as other.

At a party, man insistently saying that he isn't wearing any clothes, while he is.

ASHED RELEVANCY.

Trees, blue skies, and a bumblebee.

"I have nothing to hide."

These women in sunglasses with non-stereotypical haircolors.

Beyond kinky.

I don't make good tea.

"However, my mom bought me a white motorized bicycle so all is fine."

My favorite torn piece, like a life hangnail.

> The difficulty of fully absorbing any emotional experience and so you live in fragments.

No fast growth region stays that way forever.

Hieroglyphic fear of the unnamed.

I needed some alone time, so I took the stairs.

"I HAVE NEVER HAD A LIFE OF HABITS."

Everyone blushing while they make announcements.

Worshipping by sitting down.

If it goes wrong, there is no backup.

[thunderclap]

> Looking into our hearts is maybe not
> looking deep enough.

Doing the crazy poetess in the hotel room thing.

EVERYTHING NEW IS A NOSTALGIA.

Alone and not just in the economic sense.

Nightgown on stairway's descent.

A rewriting of King Lear but without Shakespeare's characters, plot, or language.

> The trace left behind of things that have
> been lost.

"Fear saves us every time."

The letter where the damned have holed away their hearts.

Clockwork tracings on the headboard.

The fetish required to dissolve fears.

THEATER IN PARENTHESIS.

[goose honks]

Avoiding all the upper octaves.

The losers were voters and legislators.

The despair when we realize that the self we conceive of is untouchable, unchangeable, immortal, but that we are not.

"The libidinal multiplicity."

The context situated just slightly outside
the poem.

"A lot of unusual things have been happening to me lately."

What your father says about pharaohs.

A mention of water but there is no water.

The number is now thirteen states.

"Do you remember back when suitcases with wheels didn't exist?
I met the man who invented those," he tells me.

A lot of "dropped calls" today.

The music and the wind is the water, press 4 for the water.

> The opposite of meaning is not the
> indeterminacy of meaning.

The decision's reasoning is just made up.

She rubs off her lipstick before she passes him the bottle.

"Pain is not a final destination."

Dream I am waiting somewhere in a big house with a bunch of other people waiting, and we start talking about zombies, and soon there are zombies in the house, or the people become zombies, but they are not scary zombies they are just casual zombies.

Semiotics is an occasion.

The purposeful flat note. As if mistakes and incompetence were something to strive for.

Sleep is just for a bleak darkness
to disappear into for a while,
and then we come out of it
and it is lost forever.

> Writing as an external memory system.

"One must be careful to call a predator by its proper plural."

DRESSING UP YOUR LYRICAL "I" ALL IN RED.

Sara asked me how I was, and I said it was cold earlier, but it's fine now.

Now that I know I will cross it out, writing it more and more.

Secret court orders issued to American phone companies.

"Some goddamn preacher's going to preach
a goddamn sermon over my goddamn dead body."

We are watching the sun set or rise, waiting through everything.

I'm nervous, but I'm going to do it.

The Day and how I behave in it.

Or in art how the superfluous is not superfluous.

You have to have a process if you don't have a narrative.

IN AN EFFORT TO SAVE THE STUPID KOALA TEMPS.

"Don't be all sixes and sevens."

I don't actually know why she'd been crying.

Every song happens in the desert.

The phobia beneath the anger, the violence beneath the fear.

If you want to find the needle in the haystack, you have to have the haystack.

Doubt about another's strategy of subversion.

"A story with resignation is never bad."

I changed clothes and feel a lot better.

That Jesus did not say anything against
practices of stoning.

"You look Freudian."

My mother weeping.

Nimble speech, but a meaningless nimbleness.

If our blood is talking to us.

The word digital wasn't even in our vocabulary.

"I lack your genius with the perverse."

Preferring that one's girls be boys and one's boys be girls.

MODALITY OF TEMPTATION.

It's like we're always doing laundry, but we have really amazing laundry soundtrack music.

There are ghosts walking towards me.

The reason why disarming the police is not a real conversation.

Refusing locks. Take my energy.

The poem before the poem, being the
small, compacted, momentary, subunit
of the poem.

Planning ahead shows you have a plan.

"Don't kill the goose that lays the golden egg."

Magic is not working.

She tells us to try to imagine the future, and I start to cry.

> Stop reading for meaning, read instead
> for cadencies, ambiences.

THE CHORUS'S MUMBLING.

Desire's expansion through language.

The bigger the city, the larger the racial wage gap.

Poetic language at its core a form of incoherence.

"She knew how to go without things."

A smile is a sexual symbol advertising one's state of de-weaponization.

I pretended to understand, but I didn't really.

I am the obstacle course.

V. Vibratory Milieu

A play of preferences. [prefaces].

This is not a Beatrice narrative.

If a return is a new type of progression.

Prayers left on the floor.

Beverly is absent.

"It's absolutely ludicrous how mechanical a person can be."

THE SILENCE BETWEEN THE SONGS' PARALLEL TO THE DREAM'S MEMORY.

It's stuff in the ether.

"Truth—like art—is in the eye of the beholder.
You believe what you choose & I'll believe what I know."

The pre-chorus vs the bridge.

A kindness interwoven with aloofness.

"A life lacking any trace of mystery."

The binary revealed as contingent.

"He was shooting at mobile black sociality walking down the street."
—Fred Moten

A girl's identity as a kind of loss.

> As soon as I say your name you walk
> through the doorway.

"I'm game for anything, I just want to know how much you charge."

IF THE VIBRATION FILLS THE ROOM.

"Women especially are hell to get to know."

Opposition that erases difference.

Aladdin's lamp's wish.

There was snow, and it was damaged in places.

The rising tide of the nonspecific.

Fear that if you lose focus, you lose your entire self.

What seems to be a unity is actually a subtle chronology.

Writing through waiting.

Alluding to romantic things, but not saying romantic things.

Continuous plenitude.

Unclear if I'm critiquing myself or someone else.

It took twenty minutes for me to remember the word "skyline."

There is no God except God.

When will the binary category of sex be obsolete?

Three-leaf clovers.

The few yes's obscuring a thousand no's.

IMMUTABLY FACTIC.

Fear's specificity announced through generalities.

At arm's reaching.

Full moon in Cancer hiding behind a cloud cover.

"WHATEVER IT IS, I WANT IT ON THE ROCKS."

People who leave during intermission.

"All lit by a dim red light."

A piece of string is coming off my wrist and I start pulling it; I am stitched together.

What's needed in the meantime.

> How the dream's fire itself seared
> through the dream.

On the top of a mountain, all of us holding different cleaning supplies.

That which one becomes, but can never be.

As many sexes as there are individuals.

The kink of seeing attractive men's unconscious patriarchy, and consciously submitting to it.

Simultaneously ducking and leaping.

Everyone confused about whether he's dying or he's not dying.

The sea level actually dropped by about a 1/4 of an inch.

"Your sense of humor's going to ruin our marriage."

All conclusions provisional.

Everyone against the hats because of gender essentialism.

MAZE OF UPHOLSTERY.

The desire to give birth, the result of social practices.

Gender as an activity, repetitive.

Men completely obtuse about the power differential they're
benefitting from.

No idea what to do with lace.

The robot doesn't understand what I mean.

Male poet reading a sexist line, but because he was boring, I didn't care.

More rain is falling in the ocean, less is falling on land.

Dream I wake up in a sweat and I wake up in a sweat, but part of the dream is that when I woke up in a sweat, I was all these different colors.

Theories of wishes.

How do you unheartify yourself?

THEY TOOK THE GUMBALL MACHINES OUT.

Dream I am not a killer, but I am an assistant to a killer.

All the guests were dressed as clowns.

The economic needs of heterosexuality.

"Brand" of kindness.

> After I had the key I realized I couldn't
> afford to live there.

Deciding to be straight as a femme performance.

Taking so much out of context, and then forgetting the context.

In my locker were wings that looked like nets I could wear for hope.

Mudra for concentration.

Collapsing currencies.

My list of topics to talk about.

To deliberately reverse perspectives.

Plotting to have nothing happen.

VOTING FOR CORAL, THORNS, COVETOUSNESS.

Expect residual delays.

Sex itself gendered.

How the experience of art exists within
the space between you and the art.

Surprised that my dream body remembered
what my actual body was going through.

Insisting on a sensuality of sorts while raging against gender.

We are in a big living room with a giant fireplace with wooden owls surrounding us, and we are staring into the fire.

"He won't sleep in public, unfortunately."

The skyline evaporated.

Becoming an in-between neitherness.

THERE IS A VAN FILLED WITH SILVER SHOES.

The text is dilatory.

"My country denies the Pacific Ocean."

Telling everything you need to say in bursts of laughter.

My boss gave me carrots.

"Don't assume I'm normal."

Epiphanic (incorrect) intuition.

"If anyone understands me, then I wasn't clear."

THE STAR IS NO LONGER THERE.

The reintroduction of calories can lead to dangerous electrolyte conditions.

Let's recap our fight
and refight our fight.

"elles as standing for the general, the universal"—Judith Butler

Resisting to bide time.

Called out for having overprepared for the date.

When you want to avoid the noise, you should join lightly in with the noise.

An existence that is only a relativity.

Everyone jealous of puzzle pieces.

That lacuna between yes and no.

Self-aware cultural appropriation vs unconscious cultural appropriation.

They draw on themselves to emulate the stars in the sky, as markings on the night.

Carrying our phones around with us everywhere, like our phones are our hearts.

The tables may have been turned,
but the tables are invisible ones.

                    Whether describing things that do not
                    exist brings them into existence or not.

Having lost my interiority.

SOMEONE IS IN THE BACKGROUND,
AS IF THERE IS A BACKGROUND,
BUT THERE IS NOT A BACKGROUND.

The question of whether marriage equity is assimilationist.

The only trace is a button.

Maybe "extract" is the actual word, but the word in the dream was
"siphon."

Forgetting while not forgetting, just holding it
in your consciousness in a different way.

My topic is a little bit different from your topic, but that doesn't mean
we're at cross purposes.

Progress, being a nostalgia for the past, but going forward to it.

In the middle of the dream is a memory of another dream.

                              The dark side of puppies.

OPERATION SLOW-MOTION PINPRICK.

An artificial unity imposed on a discontinuity.

"I'm like a girl, and she's like a guy."

When the real makes its way in and combines with what you were
trying to make real.

"You have such precise thoughts."

Seeing all my unreturned wanting as coming from my own refusal of
intimacy.

But this is not a Tarzan narrative.

That my therapist knows that I've never had a long-term therapist
relationship.

Notes on imaginary conversations you can't remember the context of.

The forbidden abbreviation.

A point of view so specific and one-pointed that it ignores all other
explanations.

KNOWLEDGE IS SUBSTITUTION.

The thing with why are there helicopters, no one is saving us.

The locutionary acts that create a new sort of social reality.

Oedipus's dream of Freud.

"Nobody has the time to be vulnerable to each other."

I hate when I recognize a genre's formulaicity.

This is not a solo, not a duet either.

Self-enforced public loneliness.

"Neither NRA officials nor the pro-gun wing of the Republican Party argued that had Trayvon Martin been armed, he would be alive today."
—Robin D.G. Kelley

The language of the people's new idiom created against the language of oppression.

You can tell by the curtains that it's a girl's room.

Blurred line between sane and insane.

Imaginary contact may be better than no contact at all.

MILITANTS BURNING MATTRESSES.

Maybe death actually is quiet.

"I wasn't getting serious, I'm your friend."
"Friends never get serious."

Alternate responses to helplessness.

How naming keeps us in constructed reality.

Or, naming as an act of division.

If books made me happy, I would be happy.

Aesthetic baptisms.

Cinema in the style of a documentary that is not a documentary.

Happy that I knew the true building's history.

Do you ever feel bored because you're not doing more than one thing at once?

Dream where I'm intensely gesturing because no one will hear me.

Standing in the space where a wall used to be, pretending I'm a ghost.

doubleplusungood

I'm thinking only the most casual thoughts.

Dreaming prepares you for clairvoyance.

The I's sovereignty.

Saying everything, and even some more things, and you don't know what you're even trying to say, but wanting to say even more.

Destruction is restoration.

People's real thought completely unreflected in any official voice.

BURIED COMPLETELY IN A VERTICAL POSITION.

Emily Dickinson's pantheism.

Trying to say what I can't.

Ontotheology.

Speaking one's way out of one's gender.

Every key works, even the wrong ones.

Top down showiness vs bottom up revolution.

Footsteps from above in a place where there should not be any.

Having turned off all vibrations.

> How to remain unseen is a sort of
> hierarchy.

The hapax is located here.

THEN I TRIED THE LABORATORY METHOD.

Original sin is the cause.

And I say if I can't have music, we will all die.

The myth of originality's imitation.

Parentheses pile up.)()()()()()(

Plants that want us to believe they
are animals.

Concessions are not favors.

Not afraid of not being an expert.

Listening at the wall.
Footsteps in an alley.
Violin over footsteps.

Defeated AF.

The body, a mute facticity.

To lesbianize the whole world.

Sleeping pills keep you awake anyway.

MY PLANET HAS DEMANDED MY RETURN.

Hearing compliments through the grapevine.

The soul's location in the body, or its placement on the body.

The original as a failed copy.

Purgatorial love: in between a no and a maybe.

Huge leap from dentistry to political prisoners.

The wrong solution for the wrong problem.

A psychiatrist who pouts.

Untidiness redeemed by unruliness.

THE FAILURE TO BECOME REAL.

Confusing desire and gesture.

Identity as an effect.

He will *only* give me the time of day.

Factual information that is not actually true.

A story of sounds.

Seeing the poet-friend I love so much, at the taco place I love so much.

Radical conformity, or radical revolution.

Another fantasy of something that's not going to happen.

A FETISH IS A TYPE OF VAPOR.

A group of dogs barking, surrounded by paintings on easels.

The word you can't think of, given to you in a completely different context.

The problem intensifies so you can see it clearly.

The pre-discursive found in the midst of discourse.

                                        The question itself a debt.

What I allow, in order to enact the ritual of receptivity.

The ardor of qualification.

Contested existence.

Notes

This manuscript has been a long writing project of maximalist fragmentation; 8 years of writing, collecting, and collaging bits from many different sources, procedures, and projects including: current events/news items, lines from my personal journal, from facebook/twitter quips, lines from films and my responses, poems written to music, poems sourced from dreams, writing poetry responding to friends' poems, bits from the first section of a planned trilogy poem responding to the *Divine Comedy*, lines written after meditating, responses to poetry, spiritual texts, and theory in my feminist theory reading group.

Film Sources: Jean-Luc Godard's ALPHAVILLE (1965), Marek Kanievska's ANOTHER COUNTRY (1984), Lars von Trier's ANTICHRIST (2009), Guy Maddin's ARCHANGEL (1990), Kirsten Sheridan's AUGUST RUSH (2007), Gary Walkow's BEAT (2000), Fassbinder's BERLIN ALEXANDERPLATZ (1980), Daniel Myrick & Eduardo Sánchez's THE BLAIR WITCH PROJECT (1999), John Hughes's THE BREAKFAST CLUB (1985), Antony Balch's WILLIAM S. BURROUGHS: THE FINAL ACADEMY DOCUMENTS (2002), Chantal Akerman's LA CHAMBRE (1972), Steve De Jarnatt's CHERRY 2000 (1987), Brian de Palma's CARRIE (1976), Kanji Nakajima's THE CLONE RETURNS HOME (2008), Bertrand Tavernier's COUP DE TORCHON (1981), Věra Chytilová's DAISIES (1966), Luis Buñuel's DIARY OF A CHAMBERMAID (1964), Robert Bresson's DIARY OF A COUNTRY PRIEST (1951), David Cronenberg's EASTERN PROMISES (2007), Rainer Werner Fassbinder's EFFI BRIEST (1974), David Lynch's

THE ELEPHANT MAN (1980), Ralph Nelson's EMBRYO (1976), Just Jaeckin's EMMANUELLE (1974), Roger Michell's ENDURING LOVE (2004), Kurt Wimmer's EQUILIBRIUM (2002), Joseph Losey's EVA (1962), Oxide Pang Chun & Danny Pang's THE EYE (2002), John Cassavetes's FACES (1968), Wong Kar-Wai's FALLEN ANGELS (1995), Stanley Kubrick's FEAR AND DESIRE (1953), Paul Morrissey's FLESH (1968), Rainer Werner Fassbinder's FOX AND HIS FRIENDS (1975), Wong Kar-Wai's HAPPY TOGETHER (1997), Dominik Moll's LEMMING (2005), Tom Tykwer's HEAVEN (2002), Alejandro Jodorowsky's THE HOLY MOUNTAIN (1973), Stephen Daldry's THE HOURS (2002), Robert Aldrich's HUSH... HUSH, SWEET CHARLOTTE (1964), Mike Hodges's I'LL SLEEP WHEN I'M DEAD (2003), Erik Skjoldbjærg's INSOMNIA (1997), Christopher Nolan's INSOMNIA (2002), Clint Eastwood's MIDNIGHT IN THE GARDEN OF GOOD AND EVIL (1997), Wong Kar-Wai's IN THE MOOD FOR LOVE (2000), Steven Spielberg's MUNICH (2005), Richard Loncraine's MY HOUSE IN UMBRIA (2003), Chantal Ackerman's NEWS FROM HOME (1977), Nick Cassavetes's THE NOTEBOOK (2004), Jean-Luc Godard's NOTRE MUSIQUE (2004), John Cassavetes's OPENING NIGHT (1977), Richard Ayoade's SUBMARINE (2010), David Lowery's ST. NICK (2009), Richard Linklater's TAPE (2001), Kasper Barfoed's THE NUMBERS STATION (2013), Yasujirô Ozu's THERE WAS A FATHER (1942), Paolo Sorrentino's THIS MUST BE THE PLACE (2011), Sidney Lumet's THE WIZ (1978), Tommy Lee Jones's THE THREE BURIALS OF MELQUIADES ESTRADA (2005), Guy Maddin's TWILIGHT OF THE ICE NYMPHS (1997), John Hughes's ONE WAY STREET: FRAGMENTS FOR WALTER BENJAMIN

(1992), Peter Weir's PICNIC AT HANGING ROCK (1975), Dominic Sena's SEASON OF THE WITCH (2011), George Romero's SEASON OF THE WITCH (1973), Pedro Almodovar's WHAT HAVE I DONE TO DESERVE THIS? (1984).

Acknowledgments

Thanks to the following editors and presses for publishing parts of this manuscript, many times in different forms:

Amerarcana, Issue 4, edited by Nicholas James Whittington, 2013

By the Slice anthology, Spooky Girlfriend Press, edited by Nate Logan and Laura Theobald, 2014

Moss Trill, edited by William Allegrezza, 2014

La Vague, Issue 5, "Animal Lessons," edited by Jennifer Pilch, 2015

Thanks to the following curators for allowing me to read and whose reading series provided space for me to feel out the project in a different way:

Another Fabulous Reading Series at the Long Haul, organized by Zack Haber, 2013

Endless Summer, organized by Samantha Giles, 2013

The Pond of Unlimited Facilities, organized by Laura Woltag, 2013

The Be About It Reading at The Speakeasy, organized by Alexandra Naughton, 2014

Heart's Desire Reading Series, organized by David Brazil, Stephen Novotny and Brandon Brown, 2014

"Black Radish Books Presents Poetry of Ghosts, Machines, Courtesans, and Sgraffito Permutations" at the *New Orleans Poetry Fest*, organized by Marthe Reed, 2017

Thanks to Marthe Reed for always having been so supportive of my writing.

Thanks also to my book group with Sarah Rosenthal, Delia Tramontina, and Stacey Kohut for so much great thinking and inspiration. More thanks to Delia Tramontina for thoughts and critique on this project.

Thanks to Kit Schluter for designing a great cover for such a strange topic-less/topic-full book.

Thanks to my blurbers for blurbing in the middle of a pandemic!

Thanks to Lindsey Boldt and Stephen Motika at Nightboat Books for choosing this manuscript for publication, and thanks for all of the support along the way.

Carrie Hunter received her MFA/MA in the Poetics program at New College of California, her MA TESOL from San Francisco State University, edited the small chapbook press, ypolita press, and is a member of Black Radish Books Publishing Collective. She has published 15 chapbooks, most recently <series out of sequence>. Her full-length books include *The Incompossible* (2011) and *Orphan Machines* (2015). She lives in San Francisco where she teaches ESL.

Nightboat Books

Nightboat Books, a nonprofit organization, seeks to develop audiences for writers whose work resists convention and transcends boundaries. We publish books rich with poignancy, intelligence, and risk. Please visit nightboat.org to learn about our titles and how you can support our future publications.

The following individuals have supported the publication of this book. We thank them for their generosity and commitment to the mission of Nightboat Books:

Kazim Ali
Anonymous
Jean C. Ballantyne
Photios Giovanis
Amanda Greenberger
Elizabeth Motika
Benjamin Taylor
Peter Waldor
Jerrie Whitfield & Richard Motika

In addition, this book has been made possible, in part, by grants from the New York City Department of Cultural Affairs in partnership with the City Council, the New York State Council on the Arts Literature Program, and the Topanga Fund.